Fairy Land

Color by Number

Anti Anxiety Coloring Book for Adults
--Fantasy and Magic For Relaxation--

Copyright © 2022

Thank you
for your purchase!

Claim your FREE digital copy of our
Highlight Reel Color By Number Book:

Check out our website: colorquestopia.com

Join our Facebook group:
facebook.com/colorquestopia

Follow us on Instagram: @colorquestopia

Did you enjoy this book?
Please leave us a review!

https://geni.us/cqreview

Our Color Palette Tips

1. **Colors corresponding to each number are shown on the back cover of the book. There are 25 colors total in this book, including one "Flesh Tone" color where you can choose any flesh tone!**
Each number corresponds to a color shown on the back of the book. **There will sometimes be an asterisk (*) that corresponds to "Any Flesh Tone."**
To the left of each image, there's a list of colors used within that particular image. Simply match the numbers on the images to the colors on the list. If you tear a page out of the book, you can simply use the color key on the back of the book to match your colors. If you don't have an exact color match, that's totally fine. Feel free to use a similar color or shade. Although this is a color by number book, it's completely okay to get creative and change up the colors listed. You can let your imagination run wild, and color the images with whichever colors you like and have. The numbers are here to be a guide and to allow you to color without having to focus your energy on choosing colors.

2. **If there are any spaces on an image without a number, you can go ahead and leave that space white (blank)**
You can leave any space without a number white (blank), or you can fill that space in with any color you like. Another idea is to color that space in with a white color (for example, if you'd like to use a shiny white or a different shade of white on an image.)

3. **Bonus Images may have a slightly different color palette**
Because the bonus images are from previous books with slightly different color palettes, they may include colors that aren't on the back of this book. Simply match them the best that you can, or choose completely different colors if you like. You are the artist and you are allowed to relax and enjoy!

Color By Number Tips

1. **Relax and have fun**

   Let your cares slip away as you color the images. Take your time. Coloring is a meditative activity and there's no wrong way to do it. Feel free to color as you listen to music, watch TV, lounge in bed- do whatever relaxes you most! You can also color while you're out and about- on the train or at a cafe- take the book with you anywhere you go. Coloring is therapeutic and is great for stress relief and relaxation!

2. **Choose your coloring tools**

   Everyone has their favorite coloring markers, crayons, pencils, pens- even paints! Feel free to color with any tool that you like! If you choose markers or paints, **we recommend putting a blank sheet of paper or cardboard behind each image, so that your colors don't run onto the next image.**

3. **Test out your colors**

   Feel free to test out your colors on our Color Test Sheets at the back, and use our Custom Color Chart to make the color choices your own!

Relax and Enjoy!

1. Black

2. Gray

8. Red

10. Orange

12. Yellow

14. Light Green

15. Green

16. Dark Green

17. Aqua Green

18. Light Blue

19. Blue

23. Pink

24. Vivid Pink

* . Any Flesh Tone

1. Black

5. Dark Brown

8. Red

10. Orange

12. Yellow

14. Light Green

15. Green

16. Dark Green

18. Light Blue

19. Blue

21. Lilac

22. Violet

23. Pink

✶. Any Flesh Tone

5. Dark Brown

7. Peach

12. Yellow

13. Golden Yellow

15. Green

16. Dark Green

18. Light Blue

21. Lilac

22. Violet

24. Vivid Pink

★. Any Flesh Tone

5. Dark Brown

7. Peach

10. Orange

15. Green

18. Light Blue

21. Lilac

24. Vivid Pink

*. Any Flesh Tone

1. Black	22. Violet
5. Dark Brown	23. Pink
6. Tan	24. Vivid Pink
7. Peach	*. Any Flesh Tone
8. Red	
10. Orange	
12. Yellow	
14. Light Green	
15. Green	
16. Dark Green	
17. Aqua Green	
18. Light Blue	
19. Blue	
20. Dark Blue	
21. Lilac	

1. Black	21. Lilac
2. Gray	22. Violet
4. Brown	23. Pink
5. Dark Brown	24. Vivid Pink
6. Tan	* . Any Flesh Tone
7. Peach	
8. Red	
10. Orange	
12. Yellow	
14. Light Green	
15. Green	
16. Dark Green	
17. Aqua Green	
18. Light Blue	
19. Blue	

1. Black

2. Gray

3. Dark Gray

5. Dark Brown

6. Tan

7. Peach

8. Red

10. Orange

12. Yellow

13. Golden Yellow

15. Green

16. Dark Green

17. Aqua Green

18. Light Blue

21. Lilac

22. Violet

24. Vivid Pink

*. Any Flesh Tone

2. Gray

3. Dark Gray

4. Brown

6. Tan

7. Peach

8. Red

11. Light Yellow

12. Yellow

14. Light Green

15. Green

16. Dark Green

18. Light Blue

21. Lilac

22. Violet

23. Pink

24. Vivid Pink

*. Any Flesh Tone

4. Brown

6. Tan

8. Red

9. Orange Red

10. Orange

12. Yellow

14. Red

15. Green

16. Dark Green

17. Aqua Green

18. Light Blue

19. Blue

20. Dark Blue

23. Pink

24. Vivid Pink

*. Any Flesh Tone

2. Gray

4. Brown

5. Dark Brown

6. Tan

7. Peach

8. Red

9. Orange Red

10. Orange

11. Light Yellow

12. Yellow

13. Golden Yellow

14. Light Green

15. Green

16. Dark Green

17. Aqua Green

18. Light Blue

19. Blue

20. Dark Blue

22. Violet

23. Pink

24. Vivid Pink

*. Any Flesh Tone

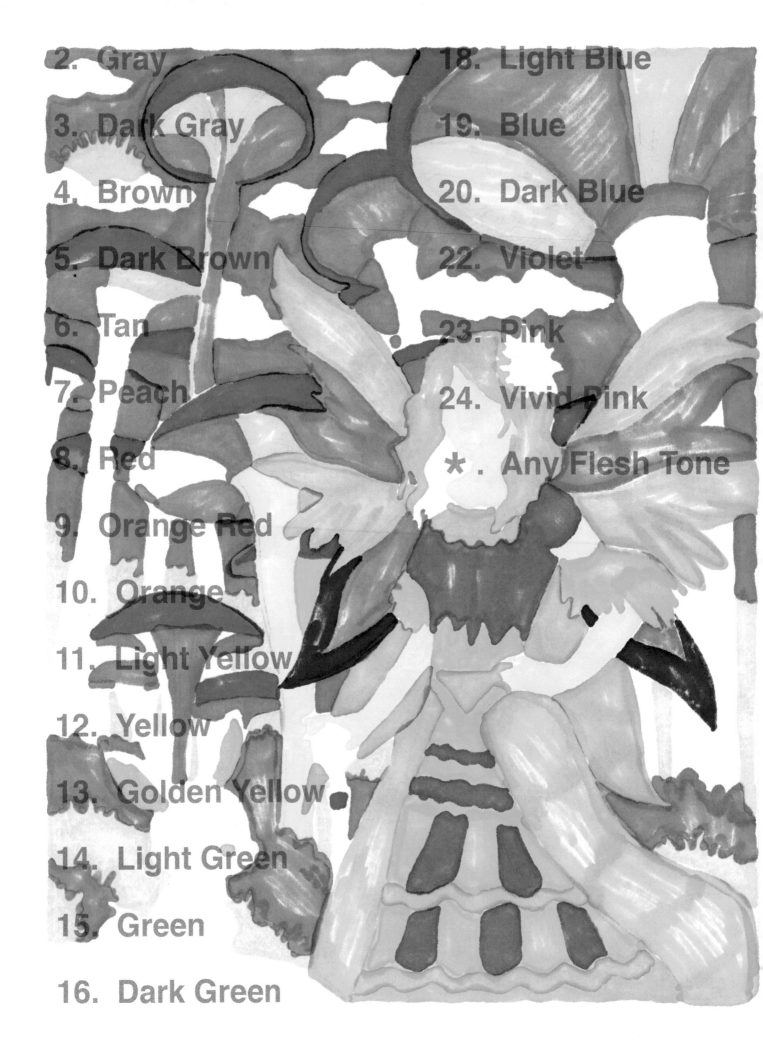

2. Gray

3. Dark Gray

4. Brown

5. Dark Brown

6. Tan

7. Peach

8. Red

9. Orange Red

10. Orange

11. Light Yellow

12. Yellow

13. Golden Yellow

14. Light Green

15. Green

16. Dark Green

18. Light Blue

19. Blue

20. Dark Blue

22. Violet

23. Pink

24. Vivid Pink

*. Any Flesh Tone

2. Gray

3. Dark Gray

4. Brown

5. Dark Brown

6. Tan

8. Red

9. Orange Red

10. Orange

11. Light Yellow

12. Yellow

15. Green

16. Dark Green

17. Aqua Green

18. Light Blue

23. Pink

24. Vivid Pink

* . Any Flesh Tone

2. Gray

3. Dark Gray

4. Brown

5. Dark Brown

6. Tan

7. Peach

8. Red

9. Orange Red

11. Light Yellow

13. Golden Yellow

14. Light Green

15. Green

16. Dark Green

17. Aqua Green

18. Light Blue

19. Blue

20. Dark Blue

23. Pink

24. Vivid Pink

∗ . Any Flesh Tone

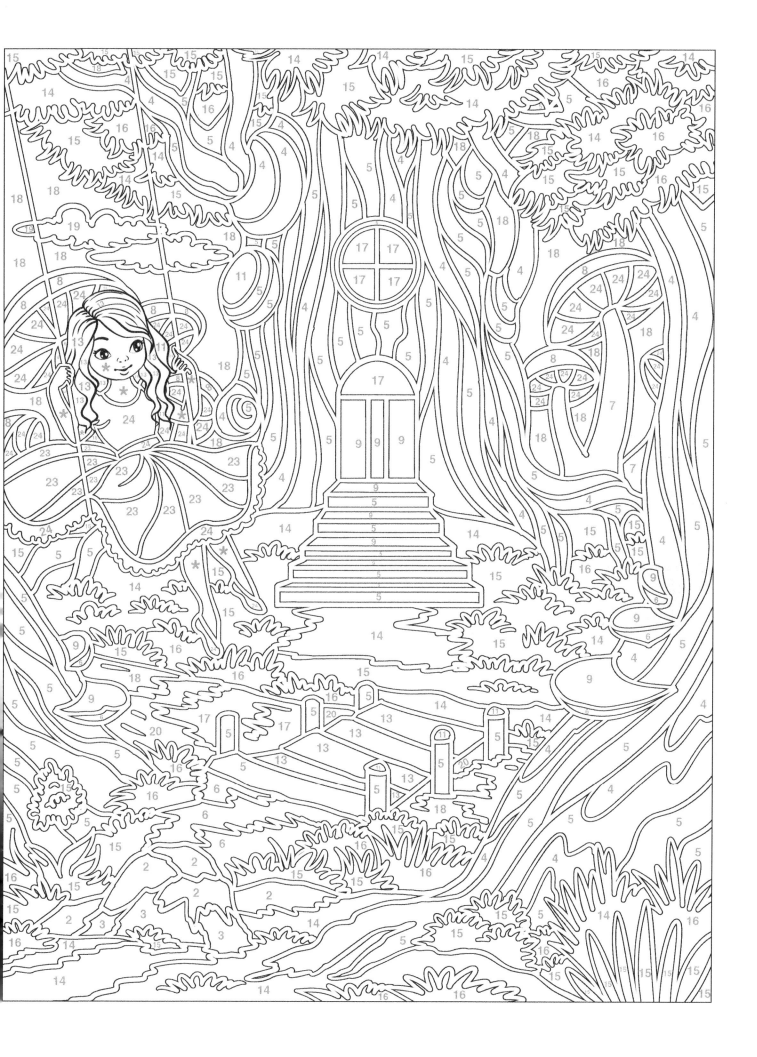

2. Gray

3. Dark Gray

4. Brown

5. Dark Brown

6. Tan

11. Light Yellow

12. Yellow

13. Golden Yellow

14. Light Green

15. Green

16. Dark Green

17. Aqua Green

18. Light Blue

19. Blue

21. Lilac

22. Violet

23. Pink

24. Vivid Pink

*. Any Flesh Tone

2. Gray

4. Brown

5. Dark Brown

6. Tan

7. Peach

8. Red

9. Orange Red

10. Orange

11. Light Yellow

12. Yellow

13. Golden Yellow

14. Light Green

15. Green

16. Dark Green

17. Aqua Green

18. Light Blue

19. Blue

22. Violet

23. Pink

*. Any Flesh Tone

2. Gray

3. Dark Gray

4. Brown

5. Dark Brown

7. Peach

8. Red

9. Orange Red

10. Orange

11. Light Yellow

12. Yellow

13. Golden Yellow

14. Light Green

15. Green

16. Dark Green

18. Light Blue

19. Blue

23. Pink

24. Vivid Pink

*. Any Flesh Tone

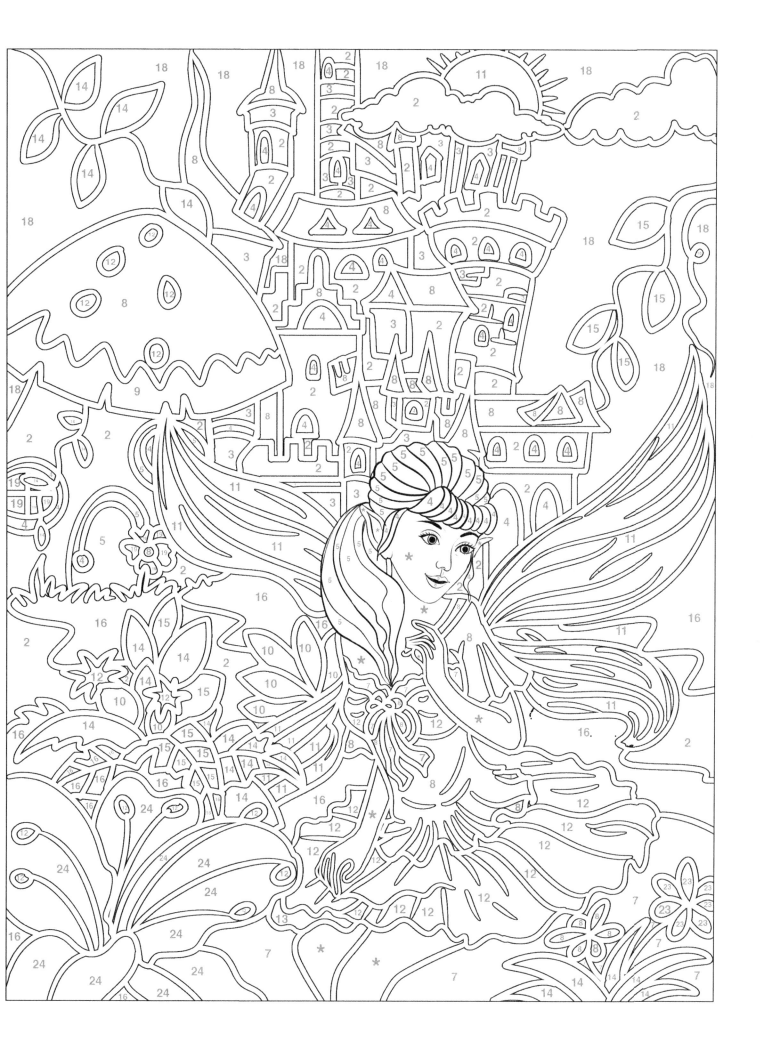

2. Gray	18. Light Blue
4. Brown	19. Blue
5. Dark Brown	21. Lilac
6. Tan	22. Violet
7. Peach	23. Pink
8. Red	24. Vivid Pink
9. Orange Red	*. Any Flesh Tone
10. Orange	
11. Light Yellow	
12. Yellow	
13. Golden Yellow	
14. Light Green	
15. Green	
16. Dark Green	
17. Aqua Green	

3. Dark Gray

4. Brown

5. Dark Brown

6. Tan

7. Peach

8. Red

11. Light Yellow

12. Yellow

13. Golden Yellow

14. Light Green

15. Green

16. Dark Green

18. Light Blue

19. Blue

21. Lilac

22. Violet

23. Pink

24. Vivid Pink

* . Any Flesh Tone

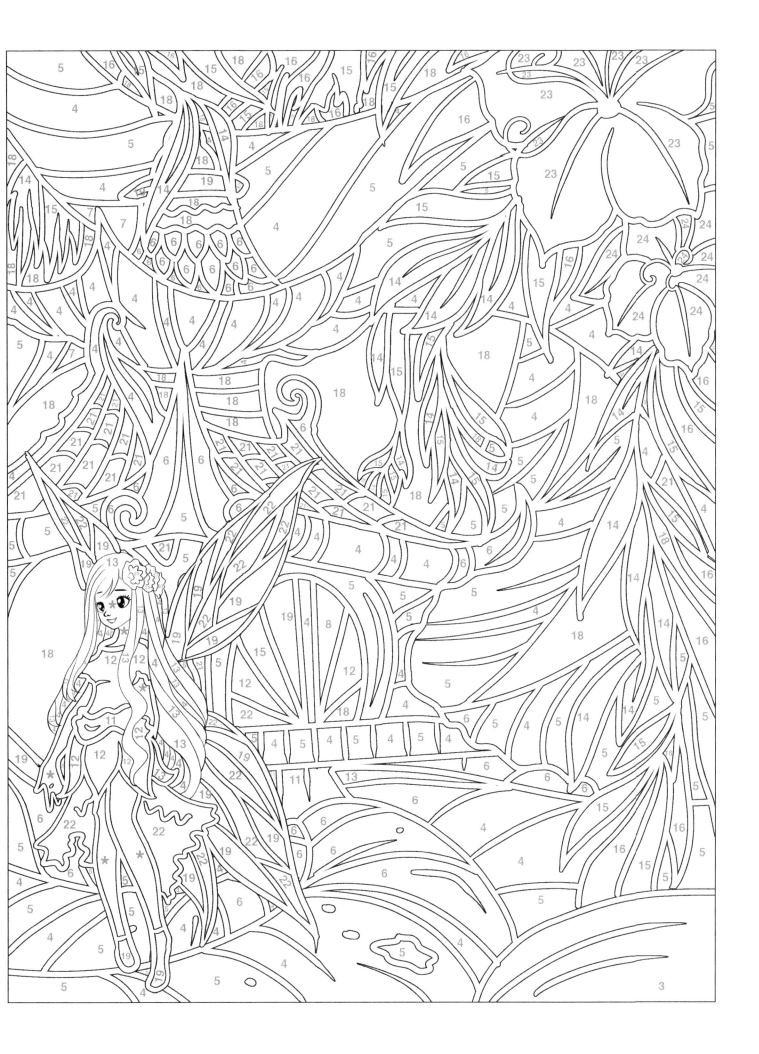

2. Gray

3. Dark Gray

4. Brown

5. Dark Brown

6. Tan

7. Peach

8. Red

9. Orange Red

11. Light Yellow

12. Yellow

13. Golden Yellow

14. Light Green

15. Green

16. Dark Green

17. Aqua Green

18. Light Blue

19. Blue

23. Pink

24. Vivid Pink

*. Any Flesh Tone

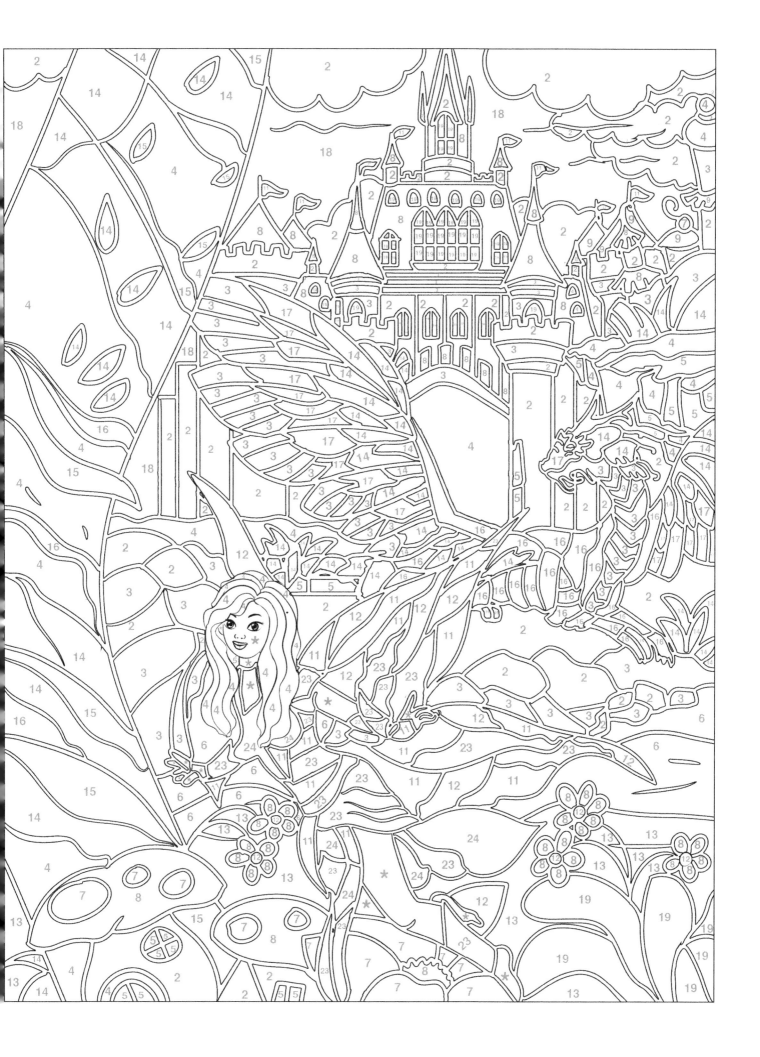

2. Gray

3. Dark Gray

4. Brown

5. Dark Brown

6. Tan

7. Peach

8. Red

9. Orange Red

10. Orange

11. Light Yellow

12. Yellow

13. Golden Yellow

14. Light Green

15. Green

16. Dark Green

17. Aqua Green

18. Light Blue

22. Violet

23. Pink

24. Vivid Pink

* . Any Flesh Tone

2. Gray

4. Brown

5. Dark Brown

6. Tan

7. Peach

8. Red

9. Orange Red

10. Orange

11. Light Yellow

12. Yellow

13. Golden Yellow

14. Light Green

15. Green

16. Dark Green

18. Light Blue

19. Blue

21. Lilac

22. Violet

23. Pink

* . Any Flesh Tone

2. Gray

3. Dark Gray

4. Brown

5. Dark Brown

7. Peach

8. Red

10. Orange

11. Light Yellow

12. Yellow

13. Golden Yellow

14. Light Green

15. Green

16. Dark Green

17. Aqua Green

18. Light Blue

19. Blue

20. Dark Blue

22. Violet

23. Pink

★. Any Flesh Tone

3. Dark Gray

4. Brown

5. Dark Brown

6. Tan

7. Peach

8. Red

9. Orange Red

10. Orange

11. Light Yellow

12. Yellow

13. Golden Yellow

14. Light Green

15. Green

16. Dark Green

17. Aqua Green

18. Light Blue

19. Blue

22. Violet

23. Pink

24. Vivid Pink

* . Any Flesh Tone

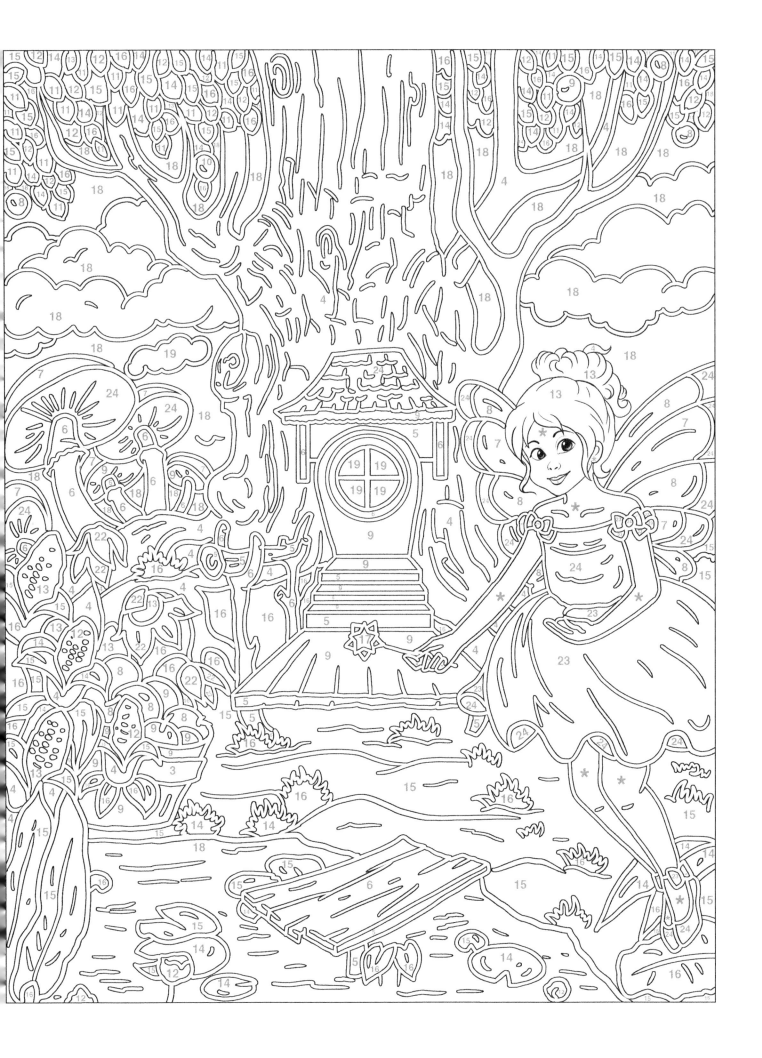

2. Gray

3. Dark Gray

4. Brown

5. Dark Brown

6. Tan

7. Peach

8. Red

9. Orange Red

10. Orange

11. Light Yellow

12. Yellow

13. Golden Yellow

14. Light Green

15. Green

16. Dark Green

17. Aqua Green

18. Light Blue

20. Dark Blue

22. Violet

23. Pink

24. Vivid Pink

* . Any Flesh Tone

ENJOY BONUS IMAGES FROM SOME OF OUR OTHER FUN COLOR BY NUMBER BOOKS!

FIND ALL OF OUR BOOKS ON AMAZON

Fairy Magic
Color By Number
An Enchanted Mosaic
Coloring Book For Adults

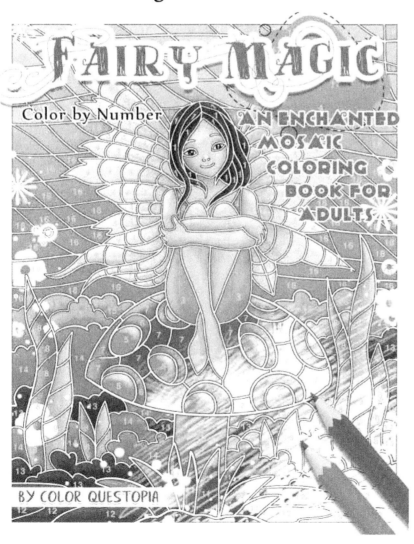

1. Peach
2. Blue
3. Light Pink
4. Pink
5. Dark Brown
6. Violet
7. Yellow
8. Baby Blue
9. Light Blue
10. Light Gray
11. Neon Green
12. Army Green
13. Dark Green
14. Green
15. Light Green
16. Red
17. Orange

Gnome Coloring Book
Color By Numbers For Adults
Cute Funny Gnomes at Home
And In Nature

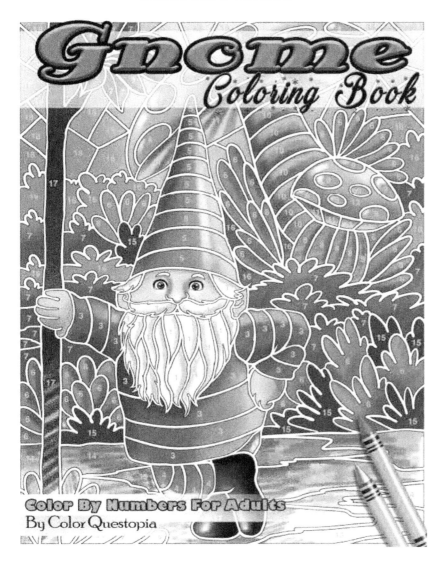

1. White

2. Peach

3. Light Pink

4. Violet

5. Yellow

6. Light Brown

7. Brown

8. Army Green

9. Light Green

10. Green

11. Orange

12. Dark Orange

13. Beige

14. Dark Brown

15. Red

16. Gray

17. Sky Blue

Unicorn Coloring Book
Enchanted Coloring with Magical Flowers,
Cute Fairy Princesses, and Fantasy Scenes
Mosaic Color By Number

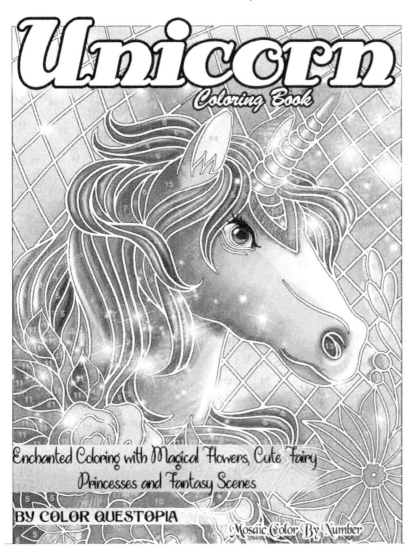

1. Violet

2. Black

3. Dark Blue

4. White

5. Yellow

6. Pink

7. Neon Green

8. Light Pink

9. Green

10. Dark Violet

11. Dark Green

12. Soft Violet

13. Light Violet

14. Red

15. Medium Green

16. Light Green

17. Sky Blue

Winter Mandalas
Color By Number
Coloring Book for Adults

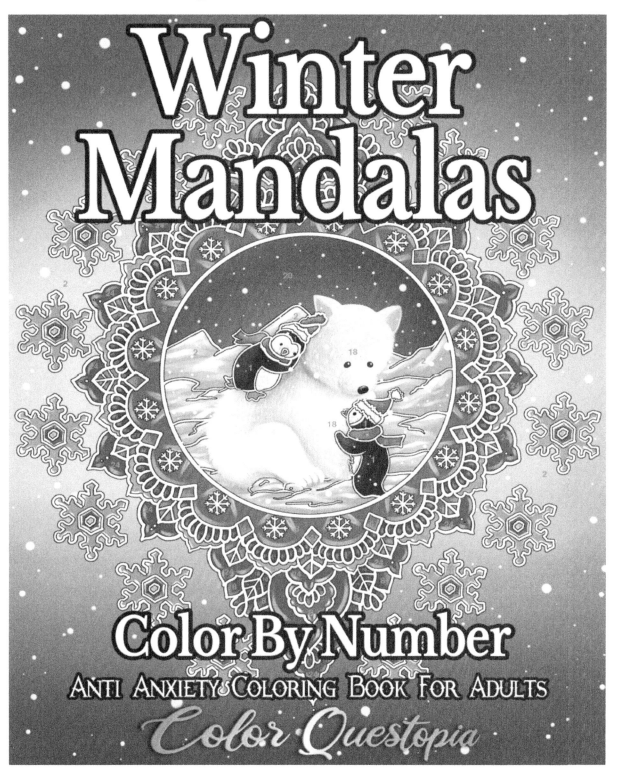

1. Black

4. Brown

5. Dark Brown

7. Peach

8. Red

9. Orange Red

10. Orange

11. Light Yellow

12. Yellow

13. Golden Yellow

15. Green

18. Light Blue

19. Blue

20. Dark Blue

21. Lilac

23. Pink

24. Vivid Pink

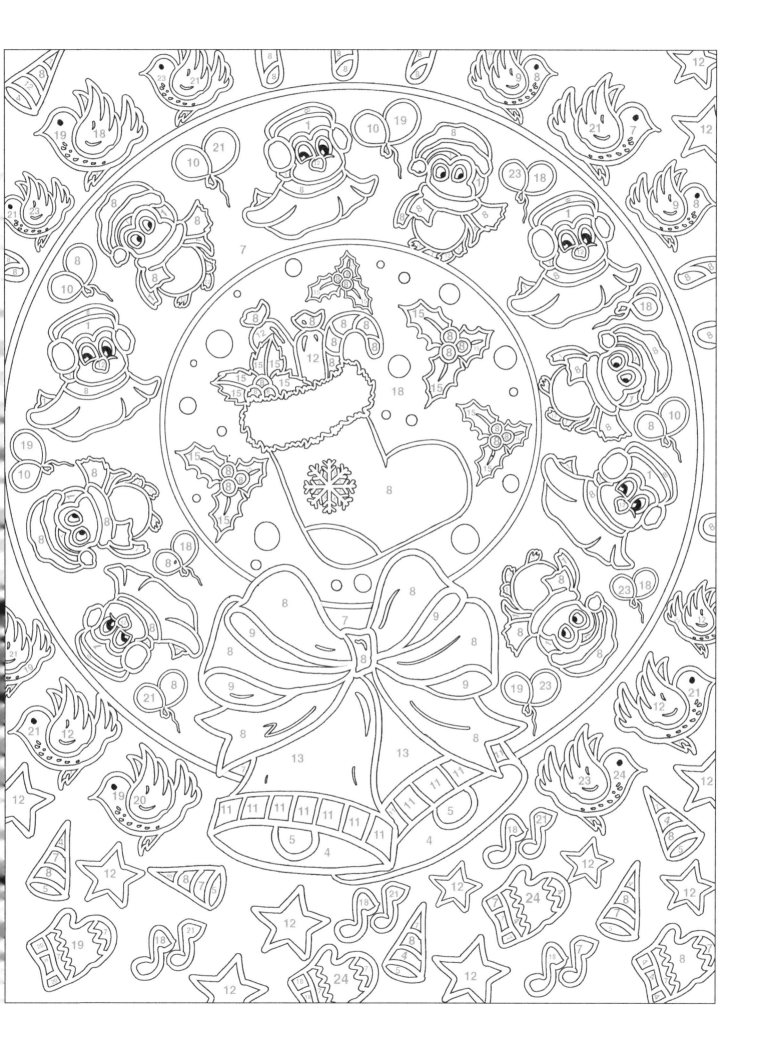

Delicious Food
Color By Number
Coloring Book for Adults

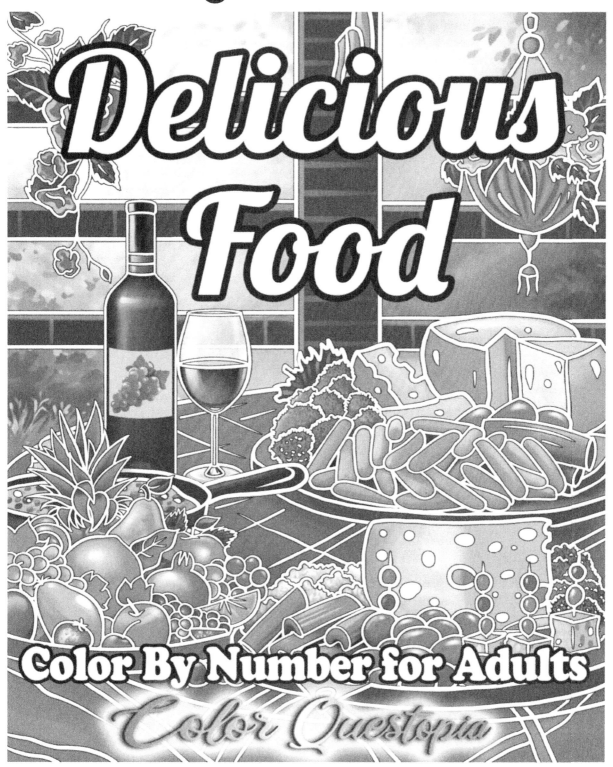

Delicious Food

Color By Number for Adults

Color Questopia

1. Black

2. Gray

4. Brown

5. Dark Brown

6. Tan

7. Peach

8. Red

10. Orange

11. Light Yellow

12. Yellow

13. Golden Yellow

15. Green

16. Dark Green

17. Aqua Green

18. Light Blue

19. Blue

Custom Color Chart

Medium: _ _ _ _ _ _ _ _ _   Brand: _ _ _ _ _ _ _ _ _

1. Black _____

2. Gray _____

3. Dark Gray _____

4. Brown _____

5. Dark Brown _____

6. Tan _____

7. Peach _____

8. Red _____

9. Orange Red _____

10. Orange _____

11. Light Yellow _____

12. Yellow _____

13. Golden Yellow _____

14. Light Green _____

15. Green _____

16. Dark Green _____

17. Aqua Green _____

18. Light Blue _____

19. Blue _____

20. Dark Blue _____

21. Lilac _____

22. Violet _____

23. Pink _____

24. Vivid Pink _____

* Flesh Tone _____

Custom Color Chart

Medium: _ _ _ _ _ _ _ _ _   Brand: _ _ _ _ _ _ _ _ _

1. _____

2. _____

3. _____

4. _____

5. _____

6. _____

7. _____

8. _____

9. _____

10. _____

11. _____

*12. _____

13. _____

14. _____

15. _____

16. _____

17. _____

18. _____

19. _____

20. _____

21. _____

22. _____

23. _____

24. _____

* _____

Color Testing Sheet

Color Testing Sheet

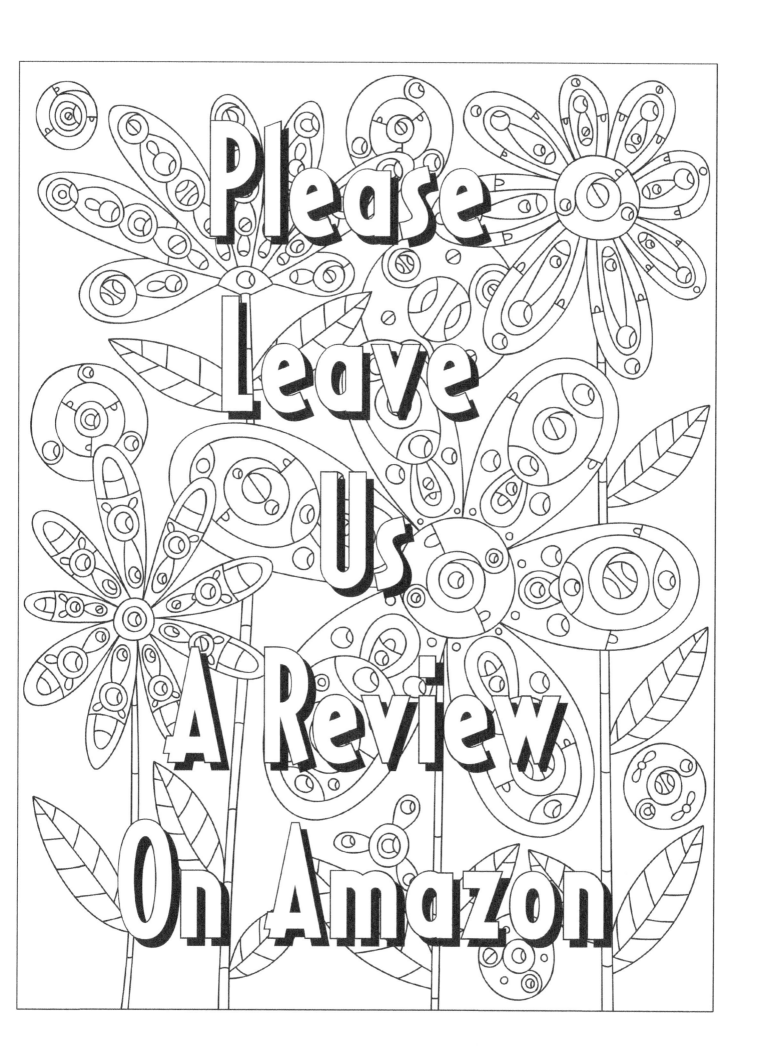

Printed in Great Britain
by Amazon

86973350R00052